The Bubble Wrap

and other poems

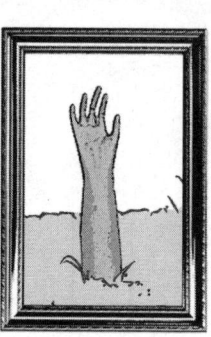

The Bubble Wrap

and other poems

Dean Parkin

Published 2017 by
Small Donkey Books
The Poetry Business
Bank Street Arts
32-40 Bank Street
Sheffield S1 2DS

Copyright © Dean Parkin 2017
All Rights Reserved

ISBN 978-1-910367-90-2
Typeset by Tim Morris
Printed and bound by
CPI Group (UK) Ltd, Croydon, CR0 4YY

Small Donkey Books are a member of Inpress:
www.inpressbooks.co.uk. Distributed by NBN
International, Airport Business Centre, 10 Thornbury Road
Plymouth PL6 7PP

The Poetry Business gratefully acknowledges the support
of Arts Council England.

Contents

9	Morning
10	Truth about the Moon
11	Short Poems of Everyday Magic
14	How I Escaped
16	The Haystack Noodle
17	How Tall?
18	The Sandal, the Doll & the Back Door Key
20	Have You Tried Looking Under Your Bed?
21	A Can of Spagnats
22	Four Friends & Six Weeks
24	New Shoes
25	Three Teachers
27	What Noise Was That?
28	The Gerbil
30	Chicken & Chips
31	Lost Dog Found
33	Pack of Dogs
34	Terrific, Horrific or Squit (part 1)
35	If You Ever Look Through the Window
36	September's Guest
38	Truth about Trees
39	First Lesson of the New Term
40	Constable's Clouds

42	Brambles & Blackberries
43	Billy Next Door
44	Other Uses for a Smart Phone Without It Leaving Your Hand
45	Another Can of Spagnats
46	The Day for a Scarf
48	The Best Thing about a Sneeze
50	Grandad in Goal
51	Keeper's Ball
52	Light for Darker Evenings
53	Five Haiku Sung by the Sea
54	Truth about the Sea
55	Terrific, Horrific or Squit (part 2)
56	The Only Aeroplane I Built
57	The Bubble Wrapped
58	Good Words to Send by Bubble
59	The Bubble Wrap
60	One More Can of Spagnats

Morning

I think I'm allergic to mornings
I'm tired of getting out of bed
Why do they have to be early
Let's make them later instead.

Truth about the Moon

The moon is a glass of milk from above
It's as small as it looks not far out of reach
It's a tablet dissolving behind a cloud

The other day the moon got embarrassed and went red
It works most nights, yawns and says, 'I'm tired'
It feels like the last piece of chocolate orange in January

The moon is as cold as a dog's nose
It hangs in the sky on a hook
In Ipswich they knocked down the moon

and it was just like the egg guy who fell off the wall

Short Poems of Everyday Magic

The Magic of the Bed
Close your eyes
and time travel
to the next morning.

The Magic of the Trees
Rotten old sticks
but as quick as you can say
March, April, May
suddenly green.

The Magic of Dinner
A plateful
but look again —
not a sausage left.

The Magic of Yesterday's Socks on the Floor
Turn out the light
by morning one white sock
and the only other one
you can find is blue
(and now you have two
odd socks). Give them a sniff
and put them on. They'll do.

The Magic of the Football
His greenhouse window smashed
but over the fence
the children
have vanished.

The Magic of the Bus
It's a rotten trick.
The bus never waits
for you to appear.

The Magic of the Spider in the Corner of the Ceiling

It was big
and dead
but now it's gone
hiding instead
probably under your pillow
you think. You check
under the bed
only to find
the other blue sock.

The Magic of the Umbrella

The umbrella gets taller
as the pavement gets smaller
to let the people pass by.

How I Escaped

Once, I used to wish
for an escape door
in the floor.

Take a penalty and ...
Miss!
One click of my fingers
there's the door
jump down
creep back later.

Asked that question in class
or reading out loud in the scary hush
or when that girl blew a kiss
or whenever I went red
and started to blush — *click* —
jump down
creep back later.

But I've used up all my wishes
and the door
stays locked.
I just have to be brave
take a deep breath
dust myself off
and go up my magic ladder
to hide in this strange place.

One day, when it's safe
we'll climb down together
creep back later.

The Haystack Noodle

words to make you brave

Sky high pork pies
bellyful of butterflies
one step, two hoots
time to take a break

Backpack knick-knack
noodles in a haystack
three cheers, four eyes
spilt milkshake

Like it or lump it
bellow with a trumpet
high five, hit for six
icing on the cake.

(and then repeat until feeling braver)
Icing on the cake, spilt milkshake, time to take a break

How Tall?

written with Lucille Renfroe, aged 8

As tall as the smoke
out of a chimney pot

As tall as a ball of wool
unwinding upwards

As tall as all of the bricks
stacked up on each other

As tall as the world's biggest sofa
turned on its side

As tall as me right now
I think I'm four foot two

The Sandal, the Doll & the Back Door Key

They tell me
when I was three I took
my big sister's sandal
my younger sister's Barbie doll
and my mum's back door key
(our Dad didn't live with us
so I couldn't use anything of his).

They say I went down the garden
just out of sight
near the small tree
grown by Nanny Jessie
from an apple pip
and I dug a small hole
with my tiny red spade
and there I placed a sandal
a doll
and a key
and went back to doing
whatever I usually did
when I was three.

They didn't blame me at first
but I didn't dig deep enough
for magic to grow and the treasure
was soon discovered. There
in the dirt I can still see Barbie's hand
rising from the soil.

My younger sister says, *You always were weird!*
Then my big sister wades in
about her sandal and mum smiles
and shakes her head.

Have You Tried Looking Under Your Bed?

You don't find the shoe you were looking for
but three socks instead
and one caked football boot (no laces)
half a polo
Freddie the teddy, all dusty, waiting to be remembered
and the cat ready to pounce
and a present, in pretty wrapping paper, unopened
the head of my sister's doll
a green sandwich stuck to a plate
with the smell that gets rid of monsters.

A Can of Spagnats

In the cobwebbed hush
of the garage, beneath
a workbench, behind
ancient tins of paint, I found
a can of spagnats.
What are these for? I asked.
Dad smiled and said, *'Well ...*

I put spagnats on spark plugs
on door joints and engine parts.
Chuck them on a trampoline to add more spring,
push one in a doorbell that's lost its ding.
Take the squeak from a creaky gate
or make a droopy clothes line straight.
That's what spagnats are for!

Four Friends & Six Weeks

Imagine four kids and six weeks of summer.
My back garden, a goalpost with no net.
Call them Jay, Sam, Mollie and me —
(I'm the talented one I bet).

First week we start out all friendly —
okay, I'm in goal I suppose.
Mollie's cross, Jay heads to Sammy
and over the fence it goes.

Second week and it's all tennis
Andy Murray is still the heart-throb.
Sam smashes Jay with a backhand
and Mollie's over the fence with a lob.

Third week picking sides for football —
rush goalies and two against two.
With a minute till teatime, a penalty shoot out
high over the fence it flew.

Week four Mollie makes us play cricket
Sam's bowling puts us all on edge
I take a swing and the bat goes flying
straight over three walls and a hedge.

By week five we've taken up rugby
or football with wrestling thrown in.
Jay's fly half so we send him half-flying
round next door to get the ball back again.

Week six and Jay says to Mollie
if you score I'll give you fifty pence.
She runs up and gives it plenty of welly
and smashes a hole through the fence.

New Shoes

On the first day at High School
I lost them. Me in my socks
and crisp uniform
hopping hopelessly

from foot to foot.

They were last seen
in the changing room,
neatly together
under the bench.

Shoes don't just walk away
boomed Mr Covey —
Someone's taken them for a joke
or put them in their bag by mistake.

Everyone had to look.
My name was all over the school,
the thought of me in socks
a good laugh.

The future can be scary
and at High School, those first days —
just think — my shoes and I
went separate ways.

Three Teachers

Young Miss Byatt
was oh so quiet
she never said a cross word.
The fire alarm broken, she was so soft spoken
she yelled but no-one heard.

Mr Beckett
could pick you up by the jacket
only put you back down when you said please.
In rugby he scared me, all beard and hairy
he even had furry knees.

Mr Cunningham was a funny one
He'd jump up and shout, *Numbers down one to ten
first one here we go! Twelve green socks
and three yellow ones. How many pairs do you have?*
And nobody knew what he was talking about.

What Noise Was That?

What noise does a bee make
    when it gets a bit buzzed off
What noise does an elephant make
    when it forgets (it coughs)

What noise does a crocodile make
    when it creeps up on tiptoe?
What noise does a tortoise make
    as it chews the leaf
        (the last piece)
            so slow?

What noise does a sheep make
    if you catch it unawares?
What noise does a cow make
    going backwards down the stairs?

What noise does a wolf make
    if its chicken tikka's too hot?
What noise does a llama make
    if it's alarmed a lot?

What noise does a snake make
    when it pretends to be your friend?
What noise do happy children make
    when the poem's reached the end?

The Gerbil

was on his last legs, half-blind,
he wouldn't take his wheel for a spin,
turned his nose up
at every sunflower seed
poked through the bars.
Dad got the job —
a quick snap of the neck, Mum said.
But he thought how the head might come off
in too firm a grasp.
He thought about drowning —
a bucket, lukewarm water, big gloves —
woudn't feel a thing.
Instead he took the problem to Farmer Bennett,
found him down a track, among his cows,
showed him the gerbil in the cage
explained, *It's a family pet*.
Bennett pointed, *Thassa rat!*
but gave a nod, took the cage, turned it
upside down and shook the gerbil free.
Much later, Dad said the gerbil landed on its feet,
sniffed the air of its new-found freedom
before the tread of the farmer's boot
spread it into the turf.
Bennett handed back the cage,
the wheel turning again,
coughed, *There y' are boy*.

Chicken and Chips

We're in the car
in the layby
by the common
when lunch is interrupted
by a fox, skinny
and limping

dawdling in the road
a car braking to let it cross.
It must be starving, I say
and wanted to throw it
a piece of chicken.
It was probably ill, we agreed,

or old, coming to the end
of its life, nature
taking its course,
when the fox returned
just as quick
with a chicken in its mouth.

It stopped in front of us
dropped the bird
to get a better grip
shook it by the neck
and then trotted off
with its takeaway.

Lost Dog Found

I meet my dog again
one night in a dream.

I feel good, I thought she'd gone,
and I have to smile to see us here

both stiff and creaky now.
Her fur a shock of white

her eyes know who I am
though she can't run

or jump up, she starts to bark
and wag her tail

still waiting for a walk.

Pack of Dogs

Cooldog with sunglasses
and baseball cap

Luckydog with a skew-whiff ear
found as a puppy in the bottom of a skip

Jumpydog that won't let you leave
without a chase for the door

Scruffydog on the MISSING poster —
found scrubbed up with ribbons in his hair

Blunderdog that sticks its head in the hedge
when it needs to hide

Skinnydog that can't stop chasing anything that moves,
like her tail

Littledog with white fur that likes to nap
on anything black

Dopeydog with two tennis balls in its mouth
that tries to pick up three, drops one
               tries to pick up three, drops one
                            tries to pick up three, drops one…

Terrific, Horrific or Squit (part 1)

A traditional East Anglian way to find out the mood of your friends is to tell them an unusual fact and ask them to rate it as terrific, horrific or squit ('squit' being the old Norfolk word meaning 'rubbish').

The male spider can't exactly sing
but on his web strums a string.
That chord makes female spiders lovesick.
Terrific, horrific or squit?

It takes a human being one hour to shed
10,000 scales of skin that's dead.
In three days we get a full skin refit.
Terrific, horrific or squit?

Scientists recently made the suggestion
that eating live locusts is good for digestion.
The good news is the average chocolate bar
has eight insect legs in it.
Terrific, horrific or squit?

If You Ever Look Through the Window

and see a web
the other side
of the glass, find the thread
spun from the centre
follow it
to the corner of the frame

and there
on the other end of the line
a spider
curled up
with a good book
waiting for a fly to call.

September's Guest

Comes round late summer evenings —
saw my light was on.
A scribble with wings
a muddle of lanky limbs
a flying knot of hair, a fidgeting italic *f*
that can get right in your face.

Six long legs, one short life.
Only a crane fly, batted away
or sometimes smooshed with a rolled-up magazine.
Instead I read he went by other names —
skeeter eater, gollywhumper
mosquito hawk

but has no bite, no sting,
just an annoying thing that still gives you the creeps.
Come here Mr Daddy Long Legs ...
I catch him in cupped hands.
feel him itch to escape
the buzz to be free.

I'll let him go out of the window
or take him outside, careful
to elbow the door closed, quick enough
not to let him back in. As far as I could see
he danced off into the dusk, giddily.

CRANE FLY ON THE WALL

CRANE FLY LYING DOWN WAVING TO A FRIEND

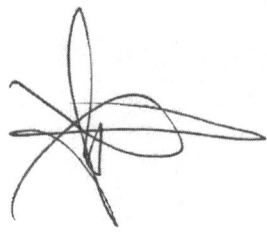

CRANE FLY DOING AN IMPRESSION OF AN ASTERISK

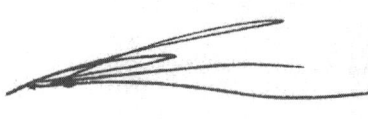

CRANE FLY FLYING INTO A HEAD WIND

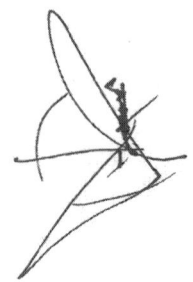

CRANE FLY GETTING ITS KNICKERS IN A TWIST

CRANE FLY HIDING UNDER A HAT

CRANE FLY SNEAKING OFF →

Truth about Trees

Trees are actually quite sticky — every morning
the sun gets stuck high up in the branches.

Trees always shake their heads
when the wind arrives.

Trees hate rain. That's why in autumn
they have golden leaf umbrellas.

Secrets are in every crack of the bark.
The roots of the tree are a perfect map.

Trees are like grannies. One tree said to the other
You need moisturiser!

If you break off a twig, they become quite snappy.
A tree's favourite saying is *Leaf me alone!*

If you talk too loudly near a tree
you can hear it saying, *Shush, shush*.

The First Lesson of the New Term

September
and street lights
mean home early
for homework.

Constable's Clouds

A washing line of lightweight t-shirts
a scruffy slice of feathery bread
a puffing bunch of chain smokers
a grumpy sheep with no legs or head

Bumpy, if you're in an aeroplane
as lumpy as our spines
cushions quietly dozing
long distance travellers as old as time.

Humongous doves caught mid-leap
a dragon's sneeze, lightbulb bones
frothy spaceships never landing
an old lady that needs a comb

Shaken diet coke froth
exploding popcorn, the inside of chips
fuzzy meringues, tasteless bubblegum
bathroom toothpaste drips

A giant bullet in slow motion
faraway traffic jams
dizzy mist, seaside wanderers
rain trains, watering cans

The stuffing of my sister's teddy bear
pillow fights that made a mess
sunsets as pink as a hippy's hair
or grey as a smudge on a wedding dress

This poem was written by pupils from seven Suffolk primary schools: Bures, Clare, Great Waldringfield, St Mary's (Hadleigh), Stoke by Nayland, Stratford St Mary and Woodhall.

Brambles & Blackberries

Like tangled barbed wire
with clusters of inky full-stops.

The hedge behind the goal
was full of them

and when the ball landed there
good luck picking it out.

Watch it! A scratch on your arm,
the football gone flat, a long plod home.

Billy Next Door

I knew the gaps in the hedge,
could push through
the tangles of branch
and see our ball
out of reach
four cabbages along.
I didn't want to crawl
but it would take a sprint
to rescue it, the ball
safe in my hands
dashing back before
Billy could get to his feet
wave his walking stick
and swear
he'd tell my Dad.

Other Uses for a Smart Phone Without It Leaving Your Hand

A table tennis bat
        A hammer for a virtual nail
                A shade for the eyes on sunny days

A short ruler
        A letterbox opener
                A stencil for a tombstone

Something to hold to your ear
        and pretend you're busy
                talking to a friend

Something to lean on
        to write down a phone number
                (when your battery's flat)

Another Can of Spagnats

At the murky back
of a very dark kitchen cupboard
behind the oldest tins of baked beans
and a box of Christmas crackers
I found a can of spagnats.
What are these for? I asked.
Mum smiled and said, *'Well ...*

you can sprinkle spagnats on omelettes
over doughnuts and baguettes
or you might make a spagpasta bake
or spagcake for spagsake
or spagnats casserole
or spagsoup in a spagbowl.
That's what spagnats are for!

The Day for a Scarf

Any scarf will do
for the first chill of September

To perk up Monday mornings
a scarf knitted by Gran to tickle your chin

To match November's bonfire
a cracking scarf with an orange flash

On a short blustery afternoon
a scarf and a half like a kite surfing the wind

For the first coat of frost
a scarf with speckles of white to snuggle in

To dazzle any grey day
a loose loopy scarf with a gaudy stripe

But when the snow is new
and you take your first soft step

for me, only a bold
red scarf will do

The Best Thing About a Sneeze

A sneeze is a rocket launched from between your eyes
A sneeze is an unstoppable train, coming out of a tunnel
A sneeze is like scissors cutting across conversation

A sneeze is an excuse for interrupting —
hang on, wait a minute ...
I'm about to ... no, it's gone ...

A sneeze is like a guitar always containing the first notes
                                                    of a song
A sneeze is like a tambourine jangling in your ears
A sneeze is like an accident in the music cupboard

The best thing about a sneeze is the echo
it makes on a flight of stairs or
how people you've never met smile and bless you

A sneeze is like a wet hippopotamus on rollerskates
A sneeze has no brakes
It can make a dozing dog or dad jump

A sneeze is a cross between the snort of a pig
and a divebomb in a swimming pool
but can hover on the diving board, not sure
                        whether to take the plunge

A sneeze is a banana milkshake in a blender with the lid open
A sneeze is a hammer meeting a kiwi or an avocado
A sneeze is a packet of crisps bursting over the sofa

The best thing is to have a tissue ready

Grandad in Goal

He wears glasses but still can't see the ball
When he dives it looks more like a bad fall
We'll need ten men around him to make a wall
Look out! Grandad in goal

We call him The Cat (an old school nickname)
He goes off for a wee half-way through the game
And if they score while he's gone there's no one to blame
Look out! Grandad in goal

They didn't have pink boots when he was a lad
He once got sent off by the referee's Dad
Our right-back's the same age as his left shin pad
Look out! Grandad in goal

He's wearing his gardening gloves I bet
He's got a bad back he won't let you forget
So YOU'LL have to pick the ball out of his net
Look out! Grandad in goal

In a shoot-out we're level (by luck) — it's 4-4
Grandad crouches down then can't get up any more
The ball bounces off him as he sits on the floor
We're saved by Grandad in goal!

Keeper's Ball

I was taught to sing it loud
by Mr Mattocks in his lean blue tracksuit
in the twilight of after-school practice.
Throw me the ball, he said. *High*.
And as he sprang up to catch
he yelled it out, *Keeper's ball!*
It was an announcement,
a prediction, a pressure
because if you said it and missed it
you were in no-man's land. The No. 1 fool.
I always knew not to say, 'Mine!' That was a foul
because 'Mine' could mean anyone. Mattocks was serious —
never forget who you are and tell everyone
whose ball it is. And in the 93rd minute
when we're hanging on to a one goal lead
and the ball sails across the box, it has to be yours,
you need to be certain, declare who you are,
who is coming to get it, because that
is your job. He lobbed it at me.
Keeper's ball, I yelled.
Okay, now try it again, he said.
*You've got a good strong voice but this time
remember to catch it.*

Light for Darker Evenings

The switch rescues the room from gloom
the floodlights beam over football after school
the phone makes your face glow while you wait
the headlights add dazzle to drizzle
the bike lights wink at each other
the street lights stir orange into the puddles
the torch finds the red in your dog's eyes
the security light shows the twisty path ahead
                              then leaves you in the dark
the candle glares behind the grin of the pumpkin
the match scratches into one small flame
the firework crackles across the stars

Five Haiku Sung by the Sea

You've heard my old song.
I woke up this morning — yeah,
feelin' kinda blue.

* * *

Noon - I seem so calm.
Invite you in for a swim.
Relax. Just drift off.

* * *

Afternoon walker —
skim a stone, throw me a line.
Or drown your sorrows?

* * *

Evening. To the sun:
You're a drop in my ocean
little orange ball!

* * *

Tonight I follow the moon
but one day I'll come ashore.
Just try and stop me.

Truth about the Sea

The sea is a fisherman, a thousand years old
It hates when people say it's blue or draw it
                                          like a wavy line
It has its own torchlight

The sea has a cousin who is a pond
The sea wishes it were a puddle
If you smack the sea it will splash you back

There's a rumour that the sea drowned the sun
                                          last night
The sea has a licence to kill
The sea has to roar to be heard

The sea is a reflection of the sky
It's cold because it hasn't got a coat on
It always leaves you with a wave

Terrific, Horrific or Squit (part 2)

The world record for skimming stones
is 51 impressive skips
and physicists have studied this
for perfect skimming tips —
the best stones tend to be brown and flat
the white and black spin and flip
and when you throw the stone
hold it back to front, to give it extra zip
Terrific, horrific or squit?

It's not in the record books
but the fastest ever duck
reached its top speed
pursued by a truck.
It was caught by a camera
going quackingly quick
Terrific, horrific or squit?

Do you think the humble seagull
knows it's an 's' away from being an eagle?
But I bet the eagle is quick to insist
'It's a completely different spelling, twit!'
Terrific, horrific or squit?

The Only Aeroplane I Built

was red as Christmas
with sky-blue wings
and big grey plastic bolts.

A present from Dad
when I was six, the pilot
had the tiniest smile.

Unwrapped
and snapped together
before Dad had the chance

to help. *I could take it apart*
I said, *and we can rebuild it!*
He shook his head, *Don't bother ...*

It landed
on my mum's wardrobe,
never flew again.

The Bubble Wrapped

For your birthday
I wanted to give you
a breath of fresh air

and I blew you a bubble
but didn't get round
to wrapping it.

I found a box OK
but the bubble bounced about
and got knocked out.

I also had trouble with an envelope
because it wouldn't go
flat.

Email failed too —
that delicate slippery soapy O
would not stay attached.

So, I tried whispering a message
into this one
and sent it by air.

I hope
you can catch
my drift.

Good Words to Send by Bubble

Before the invention of mobile phones and texting, scientists experimented with the use of bubbles to send spoken messages. Unfortunately they could only be used when sending a few words or a brief sentence and even then the words had to contain lots of O's to fit into a bubble whilst avoiding sharp letters (Ks or Ys) that might burst it.

Do

Zoo

Ooze

Igloo

Canoe

Oblong

Snooze

Baboon

Bamboozle

Ach-ooo

The Bubble Wrap

balderdash claptrap mishmash slapdash
giddeyup skinnydip chockablock shuttlecock
blunderbuss chatterbox dunderhead rumpus
kippertie boobytrap butterfly battlecry
butternut bottlebank beetlerun butterscotch
topnotch hotchpotch poopscoop hopscotch
steeplejack stickyback stickleback smokestack
bubblegum bladderwrack scattergun bubblewrap

honeysuckle knuckleduster bobbysocks knickerbocker
chokechain pennyloafer smokescreen chainsmoker
lackadaisy cherryade whoops-a-daisy lampshade
umpteen tambourines smithereens glycerine
hobnob keyfob rubadub bobajob
dawdles doodles foibles oodles
sussed crush blub gruff
gripe tiff snub hush

POP

One More Can of Spagnats

This morning, as I reach
in my coat pocket for a pen
and fish amongst the tissues
and wrappers and small brown coins
a spagnat drops out
and rolls across the floor.
What's that? you ask, *Well ...*

Is it a seed that grows a TV set?
A soundwave that's leaked from a headset?
A sequin that fell from the sunset?
Or the pin that holds in the internet?
Have I said what a spagnat is yet?
I pick it up, place it back in my pocket and smile ...

Acknowledgements

For ongoing guidance, attention and encouragement, I'd like to thank my best poetry people — Michael Laskey, Naomi Jaffa and Jeni Smith, the East Suffolk Poetry Workshop Group, Christine Johnson of Panda Books and the many school children around Suffolk and beyond who were the first audiences for The Bubble Wrap.

Sometimes poems begin with the magical help of others, so special thanks go to: Lucille Renfroe for sharing everything that's tall, Imogen Tempest in The Cut Café for inventing spagnats, and everyone at No.32 where many of these poems unfolded — my mum, Heather, and my sisters, Nicola and Donna.

I'll always be grateful to the brilliant Pierce Arnopp who did his best to teach me guitar when I was between 9 and 13. Thankfully lessons turned into songwriting sessions once we realised that, rather than practising chords and songs, I much preferred writing words in lines.

Dean Parkin is a freelance poet who runs workshops for all ages, from primary school children to the over nineties. He's performed at many festivals, venues and schools across the UK and is the first poet to appear on BBC One performing a poem on the loo. He has published one full poetry collection, four pamphlets, numerous local history publications and invented a local legend that appears in *The Lore of the Land: A Guide to England's Legends* (Penguin).

The Bubble Wrap is his first book of poems for young people.

An exuberantly eccentric imagination
- Christopher Reid

He writes with an eye for detail and a winning sense of irony.
- The Stage